DISCARD

Chess:
How to Improve
Your Technique

Chess:
How to Improve
Your Technique

by Frank Brady

FRANKLIN WATTS, INC. • NEW YORK
1974

To Erin and Sean

The illustrations are the engravings
Sir John Tenniel made for
Through the Looking Glass and what Alice found there
by Lewis Carroll.

Library of Congress Cataloging in Publication Data

Brady, Frank Robert, 1934-
 Chess: how to improve your technique.

 (A Concise guide)
 SUMMARY: A shortcut to successful playing
for the beginning or occasional chess player ex-
plaining, among other things, the idea behind a move
and why certain positions are more favorable than
others.
 Bibliography: p.
 1. Chess—Juvenile literature. [1. Chess] I. Title.
GV1446.B74   794.1'2   74-4103
ISBN 0-531-02730-9

3CAL000004059L

Contents

Introduction

This book is not for chess experts. If you are a beginning player, or if you like chess but play the game only occasionally, then this book is written for you. The object of this concise volume is to give you some speedy additional knowledge about chess theory, so that you can understand and enjoy chess more thoroughly. Coincidentally, studying this book will also help you to *win* more games.

The information you will find here is based on my thirty years of experience in chess (I started playing when I was eight years old). I've played tens of thousands of games, some of them against some of the finest players in the world, including many with World Champion Bobby Fischer. It is my intention to share with you some of the secrets I have learned.

In chess, a little knowledge goes a long way. Over the years, I've seen this situation happen hundreds of times: A player sits hunched over the board, suffering as he tries to figure out how to win his game — while he has either more pieces, or a better position, than his opponent. He's winning! The only trouble is, he doesn't know what to do next. If this player had spent only an hour studying the End Game, he might have been able to figure out the solution to his problem in only a few minutes, and with the greatest of ease.

Knowledge of the theory of chess is an important foundation in mastering the game. But as in all disciplines, theory is useless, even harmful, if it is simply memorized without really being understood. To improve your chess game, it would be better for you to learn — really *learn* — just one point in this entire book, than to skim it or scan it so that you come away with only a superficial grasp of several principles.

Contrary to the popular myth, it is not necessary to have a phenomenal memory to become a good chess player. Bobby Fischer agrees. He once said: "Ideas. I never memorize lines." It is important to learn the idea *behind* the move, or to learn *why* certain positions are more favorable than others. These are the kinds of things that this book will teach you.

The best way to use this book is to spend an hour a day studying it, with a chess set nearby so that you can work out the positions as they are mentioned, and examine them until you understand them. If you do this conscientiously, and then attempt to apply what you have learned here when you play other players, your chess game should improve markedly within one to two weeks.

The important thing is to have fun while playing chess. And if you really want to become a better player, remember that there is no substitute for serious, over-the-board practice against the strongest opposition you can find.

It's your move!

Chess Notation

Chess notation is the "language" of chess. It's an easy language to learn, and it's essential that you know it if you want to improve your game. With chess notation, you can keep a record of each game you play (this is mandatory whenever you play in a chess tournament). You will also be able to follow the games discussed in the chess columns published in newspapers, and in books like this one.

It should take you just a few minutes to learn chess notation. If you become confused at any point, simply refer to the diagram on page 8. After you have played a few of the games and positions that are described here in chess notation, you will find that you are able to follow any game, in notation, as easily and as comfortably as you read your favorite author. Soon you will be recording your own games so that you can go back and analyze them afterward, to see what moves you should have made, and to see which moves were good enough to be worth remembering for the next time. You'll also be able to study the games of the famous masters from the past. Collections of these games, from medieval times to the present, have been published and are available in bookstores or through chess clubs. Studying them is one of the surest and quickest ways of becoming a stronger player.

In chess notation, every square of the chessboard has a "name." Each square takes its name from the chess Piece that normally occupies its *file* (the vertical lines that run from your side of the board to your opponent's), when all the Pieces are in their starting position.

To begin, lay out your chessboard, and put your White King on its home square on the side of the board nearest you. Remove all the rest of the Pieces from the board. The square occupied by the White King is called K1. It is the King's "first" square.

Now move the King forward one square, toward the opponent's side. This is a square normally occupied by a Pawn (which is called, naturally, the King's Pawn). This square is called K2. Each time you move the King forward another square toward the opponent's side, the number for that square increases. K3 is the third square away from the King's home square (remember to count the home square as 1), K4 is the fourth square in the King's file, and so on. The last square in the file is K8 — and if the White King is moved to K8, it would be standing on the Black King's home square.

Now move your White King back to its home square (K1), and place the Black King on its home square. The two Kings should be opposite each other, on the same file, with six empty squares between them.

From White's point of view, the Black King is on the square named K8 — it is the eighth square from White's home base.

But from Black's point of view, his Black King is standing on K1 — his own home square. This is one of the most important things to remember about chess notation: Each square has *two* names, depending on which color you're referring to. When you're playing a game or recording a game, change the notation according to the side of the board you are referring to. If you're reading or writing about the Queen file, for example, you'd use the notation Q1 if you meant the White Queen's home square. You'd use Q8 to describe that *same* square, if you were looking at it from Black's side, or if it were Black's move.

Now put all of the Pieces (not the Pawns) on your board, in their starting positions. Keep the White Pieces on your side. Notice that the board is a mirror image: the Kings face each other; the Queens face each other; the two Bishops face each other, as do the Knights and the Rooks. In every case, a Piece on one side faces the same Piece on the opposite side of the board.

Therefore, it is possible to give a name to the file that joins the two facing Pieces. The file on which the Kings stand is called the *King's file*. The file on which the Queens stand is called the *Queen's file*. But now, there are duplicates for each of the rest of the Pieces: two White Bishops, two White Knights, two White Rooks, and two of each on the Black side.

Put your hand on the White King. Now move one square to

the right, where a Bishop stands. This is the King's Bishop. Look across that file to the Black Bishop. It, too, is standing immediately to the right of the King. So it, too, is called the King's Bishop.

Now put your hand on the White Queen, and move one square to the left. This is the Queen's Bishop. Look across the file, and you'll see the Black Queen's Bishop, which also stands one square to the left of its Queen.

Each of the paired Pieces — Bishops, Knights, and Rooks — is designated in chess notation as either the King's or Queen's Bishop, Knight, or Rook. The Pieces keep their names throughout the game, even when they have moved off their home squares.

And remember, for the purpose of chess notation, each square takes its name from the name of the Piece that occupies its file. The squares of the first *rank* — the home squares of either White or Black — are therefore named:

Queen's Rook	Queen's Knight	Queen's Bishop	Queen	King	King's Bishop	King's Knight	King's Rook
1	1	1	1	1	1	1	1

As you move each piece forward toward the opponent's side, the names of the squares in each file remain the same: only the number changes. Moving forward from White Queen's Bishop 1 square, you come to the square called Queen's Bishop 2. And then comes Queen's Bishop 3, and so on.

Remember that, from Black's point of view, the words stay the same but the numbering is opposite. White Queen's Bishop 2 square (written QB2) is Black Queen's Bishop 7 square (QB7). And White can move a Piece to KR1 (King's Rook 1). If Black moved one of its Pieces to that same square, Black would call it KR8. Same square; same name; opposite number.

The following diagram gives the names for all of the squares of the chessboard. Remember, each square has two names; one is the name that White would call that square, and the other is the name that Black would call the same square.

Study the diagram so that you understand why each square has that particular name. Practice counting up from White's side and down from Black's side to get the two names for each square. Remember: The name stays the same. Only the numbers change as you move away from each color's home rank. And don't forget to count the home square as 1 (not as zero).

Remember, too, that in chess notation, *Black is always on top, and White is always on the bottom.*

BLACK

QR1 / QR8	QN1 / QN8	QB1 / QB8	Q1 / Q8	K1 / K8	KB1 / KB8	KN1 / KN8	KR1 / KR8
QR2 / QR7	QN2 / QN7	QB2 / QB7	Q2 / Q7	K2 / K7	KB2 / KB7	KN2 / KN7	KR2 / KR7
QR3 / QR6	QN3 / QN6	QB3 / QB6	Q3 / Q6	K3 / K6	KB3 / KB6	KN3 / KN6	KR3 / KR6
QR4 / QR5	QN4 / QN5	QB4 / QB5	Q4 / Q5	K4 / K5	KB4 / KB5	KN4 / KN5	KR4 / KR5
QR5 / QR4	QN5 / QN4	QB5 / QB4	Q5 / Q4	K5 / K4	KB5 / KB4	KN5 / KN4	KR5 / KR4
QR6 / QR3	QN6 / QN3	QB6 / QB3	Q6 / Q3	K6 / K3	KB6 / KB3	KN6 / KN3	KR6 / KR3
QR7 / QR2	QN7 / QN2	QB7 / QB2	Q7 / Q2	K7 / K2	KB7 / KB2	KN7 / KN2	KR7 / KR2
QR8 / QR1	QN8 / QN1	QB8 / QB1	Q8 / Q1	K8 / K1	KB8 / KB1	KN8 / KN1	KR8 / KR1

WHITE

Now that you understand how the squares are named, you need to know how to read — and write — the symbols that stand for the names of the Pieces and for the different kinds of moves.

King = K
Queen = Q
Rook = R
Bishop = B
Knight = N
Pawn = P

Note that each Piece is designated by its initial, except for the Knight. The Knight is represented by an N, which is the actual first *sound* of its name.

The Moves

captures = X
to (meaning a Piece or Pawn moves from one
square to another) = —
castles (Kingside) = 0-0
castles (Queenside) = 0-0-0
en passant = e.p.
good move = !
bad move = ?
check = ch or +

Suppose you are White, and are making the first move of the game. If you decide to move the Pawn that is in front of your King, and you move it forward two squares, like this:

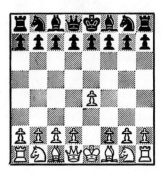

in chess notation it would read 1. P-K4

If your opponent, as Black, moved his King's Knight (the Knight two squares to the right of his King, on the King's side of the board), to his Bishop's third square, like this:

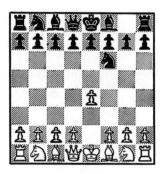

in notation it would read 1 ... N-KB3

The moves of a chess game are numbered consecutively. In recording a game, White's move is always listed on the left, beside the number of that move. Black's move is always listed in a column on the right. Thus, these two moves would read:

(White)   (Black)
1. P-K4   N-KB3

If one of the moves were being discussed, or annotated, White's move would always be separated from the number of the move by one period.   5. K-QR3 means that on the fifth move of a game, White moved his King to *his* Queen's Rook 3 square.

Black's move would always be separated from the number of the move by three periods. Thus, 9 ... P-Q7 means that on the ninth move, Black moved his Pawn to *his* Queen 7 square.

Look at the following example of chess notation, and try to match them to what was actually happening in the chess game they are describing.*

(1) 3. QB - KN5	(a)	Third move; Black moves his King's Knight to the King's Rook 6 square.
(2) 15 ... PxN	(b)	Third move; White moves his Queen's Bishop to the King's Knight 5 square.
(3) 40. 0-0	(c)	Fifteenth move; White's Queen captures Black's Rook; a good move.
(4) 40 ... 0-0-0	(d)	Fortieth move: White castles on his King's side.
(5) 3 ... KN-KR6	(e)	Fifteenth move; Black's Pawn captures White's Knight.
(6) 15. QxR!	(f)	Fortieth move: Black castles on his Queen's side.

Now try playing a few games at random from the chess column in your newspaper, or from the games in the back of this book. Do it slowly and carefully. After the first few times, you'll be able to follow the game easily — and without making mistakes.

How to
Get Started:
The Opening

The *Opening* is one of the most crucial stages in a game of chess. Unfortunately, games often begin with both players moving their Pawns and Pieces very rapidly for the first five to ten moves, until the position becomes so "complicated" that they are forced to slow down to do some thinking. Little do they know that they have already determined the course of the game by establishing winning or losing positions at the very outset. By playing too quickly, and purely by rote, a chess game can be lost before it really begins.

SECRET 1 — MOVE SLOWLY

Why should you move slowly? No, not so that you can bore your opponent until he becomes careless. And not to pass the time of day. The reason for taking your time between moves is to give yourself the chance to formulate a plan. Part of this plan will be to figure out a way to improve your position. Another part will be to develop a strategy to *checkmate* your opponent's King. Start each game slowly. Think about your moves carefully — even the very first moves of the game. Consider each one of your moves carefully but also think about what your opponent is doing. Then continue to think about and analyze the moves as you proceed through the game. This opening head start will help you to confront dangerous or difficult situations if they should arise later in the game.

From the initial position of the chessmen when you first set up the board, you can see that the scope of the Pieces is severely limited. The Pieces stand on the back row, and a Pawn occupies the square in front of each Piece. Only the Knights, which can jump over the Pawns, are able to move immediately. Before any of the other Pieces can be brought out, a Pawn must be moved to provide an opening space. But it is very important that you *develop* some of your Pieces quickly; move them out onto squares from which they have the greatest amount of mobility. Without this development, it is virtually impossible to checkmate your opponent's King. And with your Pieces on strategic squares, you accomplish both offensive and defensive objectives. You have the ability to strike at your opponent's King, and your Pieces are in position to assist you in defense of your own King, should it be subjected to *attack*.

SECRET 2 — DEVELOP YOUR PIECES QUICKLY

Move your Knights and Bishops off the *back rank* as quickly as you can. Move your Rooks to any center files that are *opened*, or which will eventually be opened by the *exchange* of Pawns. Try not to move too many Pawns at the opening stages of the game; no Pawn move is justified in the Opening unless it aids in the development of at least one or more Pieces. If you fail to move all your Pieces to squares where they will have full mobility, you will probably lose the game simply because of your inability to maneuver your Pieces quickly, for either attack or defense.

Study the position shown at left. In this example we're showing White's side, but this is an ideal position for either White or Black. In just seven moves this player has virtually completed his development. His four minor pieces (Knights and Bishops are called *minor* pieces, while Queens and Rooks are referred to as *major* pieces) have been developed to good squares, where they have command over a large territory, and the player has moved only two Pawns. The rest of the Pawns are in their original positions, protecting the major Pieces behind them.

What Is a Good Square?

In general, a good square is one that gives the greatest scope of action. The greatest scope of action a Piece can have is from the center of the board. Pieces in the center of the board can move in many different directions. They can threaten many of the opponent's Pieces at once; they can protect their own rear against attack from many sides. But a Piece at the side is severely limited.

A Knight, for instance, placed in the center of the board, has command over eight squares:

Whereas the same Knight, placed in the corner, has only a two-square scope:

Obviously, therefore, Pieces should be placed in or near the center of the board, so that they can be as effective as possible.

SECRET 3 — CONTROL THE CENTER WITH PIECES

From the very outset of a game, make every effort to fight for control of the center by placing your Pieces in or near there, and by attempting to keep your opponent's Pieces away from the center squares. The "center" of the board is just that: the geographical center, especially squares K4, K5, Q4, and Q5, and the squares immediately bordering them.

If you prevent your opponent from entering or taking control of the center, you will greatly restrict his forces to a small or backward area, which will make it difficult for him to launch an effective attack.

The boxed area is the "true" center of the board, and the most important squares to control. The dotted line indicates the "subsidiary center," which is also an important area to control.

After you develop your Pieces, keeping a constant eye on gaining and keeping control of the center, the next most important aspect of the Opening is to *castle* as early as possible. Castling is a wise defensive move. It moves your King out of the line of battle, while bringing your Rook into action. If it is at all possible, try to castle early, certainly by the tenth move.

SECRET 4 — CASTLE EARLY

As long as the King remains in the center of the board, as it is when it sits on its home square, the King is most vulnerable to attack. But in castling, the King is moved to the corner of the board and protected by a wall of Pawns. In this position, the the King enjoys relative safety.

Castling early also helps strengthen your attack. It is an offensive move in that it brings one of the powerful Rooks closer to the center of the board. This follows the advice of Secret 2: Develop your Pieces quickly.

Castling Kingside is quicker, and hence more efficient, since only two Pieces — the Knight and the Bishop — have to be moved out of the way.

Queenside castling is often less effective, though it is eminently better to castle Queenside than not to castle at all. To castle Queenside though, three Pieces must be moved out of the way: the Queen, the Bishop, and the Knight. At the end of the castling procedure, the Queen's Rook Pawn is left undefended. Should it be attacked, the King must waste a move by moving over to defend it.

SPECIAL OPENING SECRETS

1. Do not bring out your Queen prematurely, since it is your most valuable Piece. If you expose it while there are too many Pieces still on the board, it can be harrassed by your opponent's minor Pieces, forcing you to waste time and moves protecting it or moving it to safety.

2. In the Opening, the King should play a passive role. Castle early and move the King to safety, then keep it there until late in the game, if possible.

3. Rooks can become most useful when files have been opened for them. Keep this in mind, and try to open a file for your Rooks at your earliest convenience.

4. Develop Knights before Bishops. Knights will help you more effectively in your struggle for the center.

5. The King's Bishop is the best attacking Piece; placed on QB4 it becomes extremely effective.

6. The weakest point in the enemy's position is the square KB2. A direct attack on that square with a number of your Pieces will often bring good results.

7. Establish your central Pawns on K4 and Q4 when possible.

8. During the first ten or so moves, move only two or three Pawns.

9. Develop your Pieces rapidly. Try not to move the same Piece more than once during the beginning of the game; move it to a square where it can remain for awhile without being threatened.

10. Avoid doubled Pawns whenever possible (see chessboard on page 20); they are very weak, since they can't protect each other.

Two Pawns on the same file, one just behind the other, are called Doubled Pawns. *They should be avoided whenever possible.* Tripled Pawns *(three Pawns in a row, on the same file) are even worse.*

A sequence of beginning moves, which lead to a particular position for either White or Black, is called an Opening. Different Openings offer different advantages and disadvantages. The one you and your opponent choose will have an enormous effect on the entire game. For guides to the most important, popular Openings, see the recommended reading list on page 59.

The Value of the Pieces

It will quickly become apparent, even in your first game of chess, that some of the chess Pieces are more valuable than others. For instance, the Queen is superior to the Bishop, because the Queen has greater power of movement. For the same reason, the Rook is stronger than the Knight, and so on. Aside from their inherent strength, the value of any given Piece can change radically, depending on its position. In certain circumstances, a lowly Pawn can suddenly become more powerful and valuable to a player than his all-powerful Queen.

In general, though, for normal playing situations, the relative strength of the chess Pieces can be compared to one another according to the following formula:

$$Pawn = 1.0$$
$$Knight = 3.2$$
$$Bishop = 3.5$$
$$Rook = 5.0$$
$$Queen = 9.5$$

As you can see, the Pawn is the least valuable of all the chessmen. A Knight or a Bishop is worth approximately three Pawns. Although Bishops and Knights are considered to be of almost equal strength, the combination of two Bishops is usually more valuable than the combination of two Knights.

A Rook is worth five Pawns, or it is equal to one minor Piece (a Knight or a Bishop) plus two Pawns. Two Rooks are roughly equal to three minor Pieces.

The Queen can be compared to two Rooks and a Pawn during the Opening or *Middle Game*, but in the End Game, two Rooks become more valuable than the Queen.

Since the King is invaluable (because the game cannot be played without it), and since it does not allow itself to be captured or exchanged (this would automatically end the game), it is not considered in this formula.

SECRET 5 — TRY TO MAKE EVEN OR BETTER-THAN-EVEN EXCHANGES

If you try to avoid losing any of your men during the beginning of the game, and your opponent does the same, the game will go on indefinitely without progressing. Eventually, you'll both become "locked in," with no room to maneuver. One of the objects of the Opening is to exchange men — a capture for a capture. But when you plan such an exchange, keep in mind the relative worth of the various Pieces. Try to trade Pieces of equal value: a Bishop for a Bishop; a Pawn for a Pawn. But best of all, try to exchange a less valuable Piece for a more valuable Piece. For example, try to exchange your Knight for your opponent's Rook, or two of your Pawns for a Knight or a Bishop.

GENERAL SECRETS CONCERNING
SPECIFIC PIECES

The Pawn

1. Occasionally Doubled Pawns *can* be an advantage — if they can be united with other Pawns to form a strong cluster. You can then advance this group of Pawns as a whole, like a self-defending battering ram.

2. The Rook's file is the worst file on which to have Doubled Pawns, since each Pawn can command only one square (on the other side is the frame of the board). On all other files, each Pawn would command two squares — one on either side.

3. Avoid moving the Pawns that stand in front of your castled King; to do this would weaken your position considerably. It is particularly dangerous to push (advance) the King's Knight Pawn, especially if the King is standing behind it, unless you can quickly move your Bishop into the KN2 square to protect the King. When that square is empty, it creates an easy hole for the adversary to penetrate.

4. An *Isolated Pawn* (a Pawn that has no Pawn of the same color on either of its adjacent files) is usually a weakness, especially if it happens in the Opening or in the Middle Game.

5. A *Passed Pawn* (a Pawn that has no "enemy" Pawn in front of it on its own file, and no opposing Pawns on adjacent files) is usually strong. It is especially strong when two or more Passed Pawns are connected. If a player has two connected Passed Pawns on the sixth rank, for example, and it is that player's move, the Pawns cannot be stopped by a Rook from reaching the eighth rank, where one of them can become a Piece. (Usually a player chooses to make his Pawn into a Queen, but he may choose a different Piece if he wishes. It might, for exam-

ple, be more important, in a certain position, to exchange the Pawn for a Knight, if that would help to mate the opponent's King.)

The Knight

1. The best possible squares on which to position the Knight, at the beginning of the game, are KB3 and QB3. On these squares, the Knight enjoys the greatest scope, and has the maximum amount of defensive and offensive power. Avoid placing the Knight on the KR3, since this cuts down its scope considerably. It can also lead to difficulty if your opponent succeeds in exchanging his Bishop for your Knight while it is on the Rook's file. If this happens, you will be left with Doubled Pawns on the Rook's file, which as you have seen, is a serious weakness.

2. A single Knight is usually stronger than a single Bishop, especially in the Opening or Middle Game, as it can attack hostile men on squares of either color. A Knight also finds it easier to get out of cramped, dangerous positions, whereas a Bishop can easily become blocked by Pawns, either its own or the enemy's, and so find itself locked into a particular square for virtually the entire game.

3. Two Knights, which have the ability to protect each other, are very strong. In the End Game, however, if nothing remains on the board except a King and two Knights versus a lone King, the Knights will not be strong enough to force a checkmate.

4. A Knight in one of the center squares, protected by a Pawn and unable to be attacked by an adversary's Pawn, is as strong as a Rook.

The Bishop

1. Although the Bishop is considered to be roughly the same strength as the Knight, two Bishops are clearly stronger than two Knights (except in unusual positions).

2. Unlike the limitation of two Knights against a lone King, two Bishops *can* effect mate, working together with their own King at the end of the game.

3. When both players are left with Bishops of opposite colors (if your Bishop stands on the White squares, and your opponent's Bishop stands on the Black squares, or vice versa), if your position and *material* are equal, the result is usually a drawn game.

4. The King's Bishop is usually a better attacking Piece than the Queen's Bishop.

The Rook

1. The Rook realizes its full potential at the later stages of the Middle Game, and it is especially strong in the End Game, where it has full scope of action.

2. Always try to gain command control of an open file with your Rooks.

3. In the End Game, a Rook to the seventh rank is usually a good move. Two Rooks on that same rank are even better.

4. A lone Rook usually wins in the End Game against either a lone Bishop or Knight, in a game with an equal number of Pawns on either side.

5. In an End Game with Pawns, two Rooks are usually better than a Queen.

The Queen

1. Be wary of bringing your Queen out too early in the game, because it might be attacked by minor Pieces and be forced to re-

treat. This wastes valuable moves, which would be better spent in developing your material and gaining control of the center of the board.

2. In most cases, it is bad to post the Queen on the KB3 square, since that is the square usually best for the King's Knight.

3. A Queen on the Rook's file can sometimes be trapped. If you do place your Queen on the Rook's file, be careful to make sure that it has an exit, in case it is attacked.

4. Be careful about posting your Queen in front of your King. The danger here is that the Queen might be *pinned* by your adversary's Rook. (If the Queen is in front of the King, and a Rook attacks the Queen, it cannot move away — that would expose the King to the Rook's attack.) In such a case, the Queen would be lost.

5. When generating an attack with your Queen, you will have more power if you use another Piece or Pieces together with the Queen, all attacking together.

Mixing It Up:
The Middle Game

Though there are no definite lines of demarcation, the Middle Game is that phase of chess that follows the Opening and precedes the End Game. It is often the longest part of a game of chess and frequently the most complicated. After both sides have castled and Pieces are developed, there usually follows either a positional or combinational battle until the final struggle, the End Game, is reached. Because there are so many possibilities in the Middle Game to checkmate or be checkmated, or to win or lose significant numbers of Pieces and Pawns, often a game will end in the Middle Game before it has any opportunity to reach the phase known as the End Game.

A *combination* can be defined as a series of planned and forced moves (there can be one-move and even twenty-move combinations) and often containing a *sacrifice*. By "forced" is meant that each move your opponent makes is dictated by a move of yours. In effect, if he makes any other move than the one that is dictated, it will be worse for him, so he is forced to respond in the way that you manipulate him. Combinations are the home runs of chess and often culminate in checkmate or in the winning of material (though one can engage in a combination, for example, simply to improve one's position). Following are a few ways to produce combinations.

The Pin

The pin, one of the most important tactical maneuvers in chess, is a move made by a Queen, Rook, Bishop, or Knight which prevents an opposing Piece or Pawn from moving because it is needed on the square that it is located to shield one of the more valuable Pieces or the King from an immediate attack. For example, in the position at above right, Black Queen's Knight is screening or protecting its King.

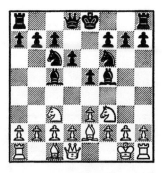

If White elected to move his King's Bishop to attack the Knight, thusly:

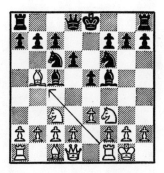

he is doing what is known as "pinning." In this case, because it is against the rules for the pinned Piece to move (otherwise it would expose the King to check which is not permitted by the rules), it is known as an absolute pin. On occasion, a Piece can be pinned for virtually the entire game, thereby making it practically powerless since it is unable to move. In addition to immobilizing Pieces, pins can be used very effectively to win material.

SECRET 6 — CONSIDER PINNING YOUR OPPONENT'S PIECES

Examples of Pinning Attacks

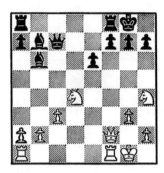

In this position, with Black to move, White loses a Piece when Black plays P-K4.

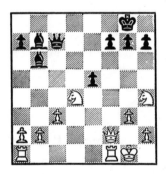

The Knight is pinned and though it can move legally, should it elect to do so, Black simply plays BxQch, winning the Queen. There is no escape plan for White — he must lose at *least* a Knight. Should he move his Knight to QN5, for example, thereby attacking Black's Queen simultaneously while his Queen is under attack, Black still proceeds to capture White's Queen *with a check* and after doing so moves his own Queen out of danger from White's Knight.

In the fascinating position below, Black's Bishop is doubly pinned. It is illegal for him to capture White's Queen as he would be exposing his King to check, and if he unwisely plays Bishop takes Bishop, White counters with Queen takes Queen!

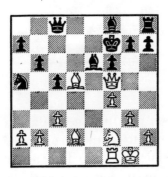

White quickly wins the Bishop by playing R-K1 and Black is unable to bring out any of his other forces to defend it. Hence, the power of the pin.

After this move, White can capture Black's Bishop with either his Queen, Rook, or Bishop and come out a Piece ahead.

In the position on the top of page 32, White devastates Black's position by creating a particularly annoying pin. Can you find the correct move for White?

White creates a painful pin on Black's Queen by playing B-B4. Black is unable to capture the hanging Bishop because if he does, he's checkmated with QxP mate. Advancing his King's Pawn one square only prolongs the agony as White removes it and the position remains the same.

Knight Forks

Because of its peculiar ability to jump over obstructing men and its relatively abstract method of moving, the Knight is one of the most ideal Pieces with which to establish a combination, especially by *forking* two Pieces at the same time. Opportunities to use Knight forks constantly arise in game after game and in all stages of chess — the Opening, Middle Game, and End Game — and every effort should be made to use them against one's opponent and avoid being forked oneself. Often, you will be able to force your opponent's Pieces into a forking position by making a threatening move. This is known as a Knight fork combination.

One of the most common forks is against two Rooks:

It's Black's turn to move and he must move his Knight or White's Knight will capture it. Can you find a Knight fork for Black?

Black's Knight is simultaneously attacking White's Rooks so White must trade one of them for the Knight, thereby losing a material advantage.

SECRET 7 — USE KNIGHT FORKS
ON YOUR OPPONENT

Positions involving a Knight fork where a check is given simultaneously with an attack on a Piece, as in the position below, are particularly difficult for the enemy to meet, since the check must be respected (in that the King must get out of check) and then the material is won immediately. There are no counter chances on the move to win back what is lost.

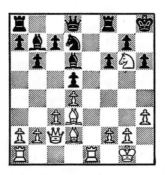

White checks the King and forks the Rook.

Other Examples of Knight Forks

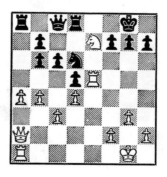

Queen and King.

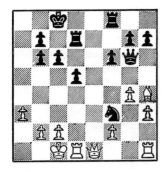

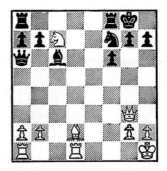

Queen and Bishop.   Queen and Rook.

Two Pawns.

The Sacrifice

The great attacking player Rudolf Spielmann once said: "The beauty of a game of chess is usually appraised, and with good reason, according to the sacrifices it contains." A sacrifice is that move in chess where you allow one or more of your men to be captured, in hope of gaining some advantage. Sometimes the advantage can be seen clearly; at other times, sacrifices can be made *speculatively* — that is, in hope of gaining the advantage at some distant point in the game.

Examples of Various Sacrifices:

QUEEN SACRIFICE

White, on the move, plays:

1. QxP ch!   PxQ
2. B-K5 ch   R-B3
3. BxR mate

ROOK SACRIFICE

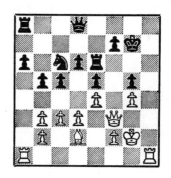

White, on the move, plays:

1. R-R7 ch!   KxR
2. QxP ch   K-R1
3. R-R1 ch   R-R3
4. RxR mate

BISHOP SACRIFICE

White, on the move, plays:

   1. BxP ch!   KxB
   2. Q-R5 ch   K-N1
   3. N-N6 !   Black resigns

Black's position is hopeless.
If he tries . . . PxN, White mates
him with RxR. *White is also*
threatening mate with Q-R8.

KNIGHT SACRIFICE

White, on the move, plays:
1. NxP! Threatening 2. N-B7 mate
   1. ...   PxN
   2. BxP ch   R-N2

3.	BxP !	K-N1
4.	B(N6)xR	QxB
5.	BxR	B-Q3 ch
6.	P-B4	Q-N3
7.	R/B2-K2	KxB
8.	R-K6	Q-B7 ch
9.	R/K1-K2	Q-QB4
10.	Q-R6 ch and wins.	

Finishing Up:
The Ending

Though the End Game may appear to be the simplest part of a game of chess, it is really the most difficult for beginners to master. A lack of knowledge of End Game principles is a constant source of frustration for the inexperienced player, and it is for this reason that you should make the ending a special source of study. The following mates are almost *required knowledge* in order to play even a passable game of chess. They are, in effect, what the scales are to music.

SECRET 8 — STUDY THE END GAME

King and Queen against King

This is the simplest of checkmates. All you need to do is force your opponent's King to the nearest side of the board, and then bring up your own King. Checkmate will soon follow. You must be careful, however, not to *stalemate* your opponent, as this is a dangerous possibility because of the great power of the Queen. *In this position, with White to move, checkmate can be effected in two moves:*

1. Q-R7   KQ1
2. Q-Q7 mate

Note that if White had moved his King to Q6, it would have been a stalemate, since Black would have had no legal move. Also, in the position at left, if Black were to move instead of White, the Black King would have been stalemated for the same reason.

King and Rook against King

This is also an easy checkmate, though not quite as easy as the preceding example. Again, the method lies in driving the opposing King to the edge of the board.

With White to play, he would move like this:

1.	R-R7	K-B1
2.	K-K2	K-N1
3.	R-R7	K-B1
4.	K-K3	K-K1
5.	K-K4	K-Q1
6.	K-Q5	K-B1
7.	K-Q6	K-N1
8.	R-R7	K-B1
9.	R-KN7	K-N1
10.	K-B6	K-R1
11.	K-N6	K-N1
12.	R-N8 mate.	

King and Two Bishops against King

In the case of two Bishops against a King, the Bishops can force checkmate, but in addition to maneuvering the King to the side of the board, they must deliver the final mate when the King is in one of the corners. This checkmate is slightly more tricky than the Queen or Rook mate, but with a little practice you will master it easily.

White forces
checkmate in the
following way:

1.	B-KR3	K-Q1
2.	B-B4	K-K2
3.	K-K2	K-B2
4.	K-B3	K-K2
5.	B-B5	K-B3
6.	K-N4	K-K2
7.	K-N5	K-Q1
8.	K-B6	K-K1
9.	B-B7	K-B1
10.	B-Q7	K-N1
11.	K-N6	K-B1
12.	B-Q6 ch	K-N1
13.	B-K6 ch	K-R1
14.	B-K5 mate	

King, Bishop, and Knight against King

Checkmating with Knight and Bishop is the most difficult of forced mates, and most players are unable to figure out how to do it by themselves. Study the solution below, and go over it as many times as you need to in order to know it by heart. As you will see, this ending demonstrates the perfect harmony of Pieces — the King, Knight, and Bishop all working together.

White forces the issue like this:

1.	N-B7 ch	K-N1
2.	B-K4	K-B1
3.	B-R7	K-K1
4.	N-K5	K-B1
5.	N-Q7 ch	K-K1
6.	K-K6	K-Q1
7.	K-Q6	K-K1
8.	B-N6 ch	K-Q1
9.	N-B5	K-B1
10.	B-B7	K-Q1
11.	N-N7 ch	K-B1
12.	K-B6	K-N1
13.	K-N6	K-B1
14.	B-K6 ch	K-N1
15.	N-B5	K-R1
16.	B-Q7	K-N1
17.	N-R6 ch	K-R1
18.	B-B6 mate	

King and Pawn Endings

Because there are no Pieces involved, beginners often feel that Pawn endings are simple to learn. They're not. Pawn endings are rampant with finesse, and you should take your time in studying them carefully. Here are a few examples:

Obviously, if White can Queen the Pawn, he can win the game. But in this position it all depends on who has the move. If it's White's move, the game is drawn since if he moves away from the Pawn, Black will capture it. And if White tries to protect his Pawn, Black is stalemated.

If Black is on the move, however, White wins in the following way.

1. ...   K-K2
2. K-B7   ...

Now White controls the Queening square and Black is unable to stop the Pawn from advancing and becoming a Queen.

In the position below, White wins whether it's his move or not, since if the Black King moves to Q1, for example, then White moves his King to B6 and then controls the Queening square. If the Black King moves to B1, then White moves to Q7 and controls it in that way. If it's White's move, he moves his King to Q6 (or B6), Black confronts him by moving to Q1 (or B1), and then the following occurs:

1. P-K6   K-Q1
2. P-K7   K-B7
3. K-Q7 and the Pawn Queens on the next move.

The Opposition

When the two opposing Kings stand on the same rank, file, or *diagonal*, and are separated from each other by an odd number of squares, they are said to be in *opposition*. If there is only one square between them, they are in direct opposition. It is important to understand the theory of the opposition because the success or failure of so many End Games depends on who holds or relinquishes the opposition. If you hold the opposition, you can force the other King into the squares you want.

If it is Black's move in this position, then White holds the opposition and vice versa. If Black retreats, White can advance holding the position. If Black moves to the side, so does White, still holding the position as it is.

A practical example of how the opposition works in the End Game is shown below. If it is White's move, he gains the opposition and with it he can eventually Queen the Pawn, thusly: 1. K-K5, K-Q2; 2. K-B6, K-Q3; 3. P-K4ch, K-Q2; 4. K-B7 and White gains control of the Queening square and the Pawn can enter freely.

However, if White had pushed the Pawn on his first move, then Black, moving to KB2, would have gained the opposition and there would be no way to force the Pawn to the Queening square; hence, the game would be drawn.

GENERAL SECRETS OF THE END GAME

---

1. The King is a strong Piece in the End Game and should be used if the Queens are off the board. Move the King to the center of the board or to the center of the action.

2. If you are behind in Pawns, exchange Pawns but not Pieces.

3. Rooks should be placed behind — not in front of — Passed Pawns, whether they are yours or your opponents.

4. Passed Pawns should be advanced quickly. Try to Queen them.

5. Knights are best in closed positions; Bishops can move more readily in open positions.

6. Place your Pawns on squares of the opposite color from those that your Bishop moves; conversely, place your connected Pawns on squares of the *same* color that your opponent's Bishop moves (to cut down the number of squares on which he can maneuver).

7. Place your Rooks on the seventh rank when at all possible.

8. Doubled, Tripled, Isolated, and *Backward* Pawns are weak.

9. Connected Passed Pawns are very strong.

10. Without Pawns on the board, you must be at least a Rook ahead in order to mate.

The Key to Success:
How to Improve

Chess is, above all, a contest between two intellects, but the personal and human element keeps intruding in the game. What makes the difference between a winner and a loser in chess, assuming that both partners have roughly the same intelligence? Certainly, one of the major factors is each person's fighting spirit, and the amount of each player's will to win. If it is *important* for you to win a game of chess, and if you are willing to combine this zeal with practice and study, you'll become a good player who is difficult to defeat. Dr. Emanuel Lasker, one of the greatest players of all time, said that it should take approximately 200 hours to "mold" a totally inexperienced player into a master. That really isn't very much time to become highly proficient at a new skill. Lasker figured a certain amount of time was necessary to learn each aspect of the game:

Rules of Play, and exercises	5 hours
Elementary endings	5 hours
Some openings	10 hours
Combinations	20 hours
Position play	40 hours
Play and analysis	120 hours

If you approach the game with a study plan similar to the one above, and if you attempt to remain as adaptable and pliable as possible in all chess situations that arise on the board, you will undoubtedly become a strong player.

Remember, one of the great delights of the game of chess is that there is no element of luck. You are the commander-in-chief of all your forces, and you start out fighting a battle that is exactly equal in force, space, time, and other factors. Chess depends on *you* and your intelligence, imagination, perseverance, and your motivation to win.

Good luck!

General Hints On How to Improve Your Game

1. Make sure before you begin the game that all the Pieces on both your side and your opponent's are set up correctly.

2. Always have a plan in mind — however vague or obscure — on how to checkmate your opponent. Making a move in chess, without any larger purpose, is pointless.

3. Before making *any* move in a game, no matter how obvious a position may seem, consider these three questions:

    a. What is my opponent threatening?

    b. How can I improve my position?

    c. What is my plan?

4. Whenever possible, play with strong players, and study their approach to the game.

5. Play the board, not the man. That is, never make a move that you "think" your opponent will be unable to understand. Always presume that if the position contains a winning move, somehow your opponent will find it, even if you have played him a thousand games and are certain you know his capabilities. Assume that everyone you play has the ability of a world champion, and that your slightest mistake will be ruthlessly punished.

6. Play according to the rules of chess and *never* take back a move you have made or allow your opponent to do so.

7. Don't move immediately until after you have studied the board for a long time with intense concentration. Consider what the position will look like after you have made the move you have selected, and attempt to figure out what move your opponent will make.

8. Learn to play with both the White and the Black Chessmen.

9. When you have lost a game that you feel you should have won, play it again and study it to determine where you went wrong.

10. Avoid playing with very weak players whom you beat game after game. If they are the only players available, insist that you "spot" them a Piece; that is, that you remove either one of your Knights, Bishops, or Rooks before the game begins, and play without that Piece. If they are very weak, play them without your

Queen. This will give you more incentive to try to win, as the forces will then be more equal. It will also make you concentrate on the game so that you won't make careless mistakes. Getting into the habit of moving carelessly is one of the best ways to become a poor player.

11. Sometimes you can weaken your opponent's attack by exchanging Pieces; i.e., by capturing his Pieces or Pawns, and allowing your opponent to capture your Pieces or Pawns that have the same relative value.

12. Learn to play all of your Pieces equally well. Don't favor your Knights as opposed to your Bishops, for example, simply because you "like" them.

13. Always look for several alternative moves and consider each of them carefully before making what seems the "obvious" move.

14. If you see a weakness in your opponent's position, such as a backward Pawn, an ill-placed Knight, or an uncastled King, strive to find a way to exploit the weakness to your advantage.

15. Coordinate the movements of your Pieces. Using only one Piece to attack is usually futile, and the attack often fades out.

16. Try to gain the initiative at every possible opportunity, but naturally without damage to your position.

17. Avoid premature attacks with the Queen.

18. When you are about to capture one of your opponent's Pieces, do not make the capture quickly, but rather look to see if a more important move can be made. This must be done, of course, without allowing the opponent's Piece to escape capture.

19. If your opponent offers you a Pawn or a Piece for "nothing," be very careful before you accept it. It might be a trap.

20. Truly strong moves are often difficult to find. Play carefully and with deliberation, and check and recheck your conclusions. *Never* make a hasty move, even if you see mate on the move. Make *sure!*

21. Try to have as much patience as possible. Even the greatest players in history lost many, many games before they began winning consistently. In a poor position, try not to lose heart. In a superior position, never become over-confident.

22. Try to gain *time* on your opponent. Try to force him to waste time, defending a Piece, attempting to extricate a Bishop you have blocked, etc. In chess, having more *time* than your opponent is one of the most crucial elements in consistent winning.

23. When playing a stronger player, ask him, after the game, to show you where you went wrong.

24. Play over master games. This is one of the surest ways of increasing your skill in chess, as it serves as a catalyst to gaining new ideas and new insights into the game.

25. Remember: No one ever won a game by resigning. Playing a game, even a "lost" game, through to its conclusion is one of the best ways to learn to play the End Game and to learn the techniques of mating. You can learn this even if it is you who are being mated. Watch and remember. Someday, you'll have the winning position; but you can't win the game if you don't know how to do the actual mate.

Glossary

Attack: an offensive action against one's opponent.

Back Rank: the first rank, on which each player's Pieces originally start.

Backward Pawn: a Pawn that is one or more squares behind the Pawns on its adjacent squares. It is usually a weakness, as the Backward Pawn cannot be protected by its adjacent Pawns.

Castling: when the King is moved to the corner of the board and protected by a wall of Pawns.

Checkmate: a situation in which the opposing King is under attack and cannot escape from the attack. Checkmate is the object of the game of chess.

Combination: a series of moves serving one specific aim, often containing a sacrifice.

Develop: to develop a Piece is to move it from its original square to one more favorable for attack or defense.

Diagonal: a row of squares running obliquely or slantwise across the board. The shortest diagonal contains two squares; the longest contains eight.

Discovered Check: when an obstructing Piece or Pawn is moved out of the way of another Piece, putting the opposing King in check, the manuever is called a "discovered check" or a "discovery."

Double Check: a check created by two Pieces simultaneously.

Doubled Pawns: two Pawns of the same color on the same file.

En Prise: a French expression meaning "in taking" — when a Piece or a Pawn is under direct attack and is left unprotected, it is said to be *en prise* (pronounced *en-pree*).

End Game: closing stage of the game. The attack is concentrated on the opposing King and most of the Pieces on both sides have been eliminated.

Exchange, The: in trading Pieces, specifically the Rook for the Knight or the Rook for the Bishop, the player who gives up the Rook is said to have "lost the exchange," while the player who gives up the Knight or Bishop is said to have "won the exchange."

Fianchetto: the development of the Bishop to N2 after the move P-N3 has been made.

File: any of the eight rows of squares running vertically between the two players.

Fork: a double attack, made in different directions, which can be made by any Piece or Pawn.

Gambit: an opening maneuver in which a Pawn or Piece is sacrificed in order to obtain a better position or to establish an attack.

Initiative: whoever has the advantage of action, time, or space is said to have the initiative.

Isolated Pawn: a Pawn that has no Pawn of the same color on either of its adjacent files.

J'Adoube: a French expression meaning "I adjust" (pronounced *zha-doob*). This expression is used to notify one's opponent that you intend to touch a man not to move it, but to adjust its position in the square.

Major Pieces: Queens and Rooks.

Material: another name for chessmen.

Middle Game: that section of the game of chess that occurs between the Opening and the End Game.

Minor Pieces: Bishops and Knights.

Open File: a file unoccupied by any Pawns, either of the same or opposite color.

Opening: a type of game where Pawns play little part, and Piece play predominates.

Opposition: a situation in which the two opposing Kings stand on the same rank, file, or diagonal, and are separated from each other by an odd number of squares, which enables the one who does not have the move to make the other King give way.

Passed Pawn: a Pawn that has no enemy Pawns on either the same or adjacent files.

Pin: move made by major or minor Pieces to prevent opposing Piece or Pawn from moving.

Rank: any of the eight rows of squares running straight across the chessboard in a horizontal manner. The rank nearest to either player is referred to as the "first" rank.

Sacrifice: allowing one or more Pieces or Pawns to be captured in the hope of gaining an immediate or future advantage.

Stalemate: a situation in which the only possible move a King who is not in check can make is to move to a square where he will be in check. Since it is illegal for the King to move into check, he is thus "stalemated" and the game is considered a draw.

Tempo: a move or turn to play which is considered as a unit of time. When one makes a useless move, he is said to "lose a tempo"; and conversely, when a player makes a superior move and "gains a tempo," he is said to have gained an extra move.

Tripled Pawns: three Pawns of the same color on the same file.

Other Books
to Read

General Instruction

Coles, R. N. *Dynamic Chess*. New York: David McKay, 1956.
Evans, Larry. *Chess Catechism*. New York: Simon & Schuster, 1970.
Kmoch, Hans. *Pawn Power in Chess*. New York: David McKay, 1959.
Kotov, Alexander. *Think Like a Grandmaster*. Dallas, Texas: Chess Digest, 1971.
Lasker, Emanuel. *Lasker's Manual of Chess*. New York: Dover Books, 1960.
Leeming, Joseph. *The First Book of Chess*. New York: Franklin Watts, 1953.
Nimzovich, Aron. *My Praxis*. New York: David McKay, 1964.
————. *My System*. New York: David McKay, 1964.
Saidy, Anthony. *The Battle of Chess Ideas*. Dallas, Texas: Chess Digest, 1972.
Spielmann, Rudolf. *The Art of Sacrifice in Chess*. New York: David McKay, 1951.

Opening

Freeborough, E. and Ranken, C. E. *Chess Openings: Ancient and Modern*. New York: Hippocrene Books, 1974.
Horowitz, I. A. *Chess Openings: Theory and Practice*. New York: Simon & Schuster, 1964.
Korn, Walter. *Modern Chess Openings* (11th ed.). New York: Pitman Publishing, 1972.
Lombardy, William. *Modern Chess Opening Traps*. New York: David McKay, 1972.

Middle Game

DuMont, J. *The Basis of Combination in Chess*. New York: David McKay, 1954.

Fine, Reuben. *The Middle Game in Chess.* New York: David McKay, 1952.

Horowitz, I. A. *How to Win in the Middle Game in Chess.* New York: David McKay, 1955.

End Game

Chernev, Irving. *Practical Chess Endings.* New York: Simon & Schuster, 1959.

Fine, Reuben. *Basic Chess Endings.* New York: David McKay, 1941.

Tattersall, C. E. C. *A Thousand Chess Endings* (2 vol.). New York: Hippocrene Books, 1974.

Game Collections, Biography, and Chess Lore

Brady, Frank. *Profile of a Prodigy: The Life and Games of Bobby Fischer.* New York: David McKay, 1973.

Fischer, Bobby. *My 60 Memorable Games.* New York: Simon & Schuster, 1969.

Gligoric, Svetozar and Wade, Richard. *The World's Chess Championship.* London: Basford, 1972.

Horowitz, I. A. *The World Chess Championship: A History.* New York: Macmillan, 1973.

Lange, Max. *The Chess Genius of Paul Morphy.* New York: Hippocrene Books, 1974.

Larsen, Bent. *Larsen's Selected Games of Chess.* New York: David McKay, 1970.

Reti, Richard. *Masters of the Chessboard.* New York: Pitman Publishing, 1954.

Schonberg, Harold C. *Grandmasters of Chess.* New York and Philadelphia: J. B. Lippincott, 1973.

Soltis, Andrew. *The Best Chess Games of Boris Spassky.* New York: David McKay, 1973.

Index

About the Author

Frank Brady has been playing chess since he was eight years old. At seventeen he played in his first formal tournament and for the past twenty years he has been a chess writer, editor, historian, teacher, and referee. In 1960 he won the Metropolitan Chess League Open Championship and in team matches for the league he was rated just slightly behind his frequent opponent, Bobby Fischer.

Recently the World Chess Federation awarded Mr. Brady the title of international judge. He is the author of a number of books on chess, including one on the life and games of Bobby Fischer.